LOOK BOOKS

LOOK AT CHURCHES

Other titles in this series are

Look at Castles
ALFRED DUGGAN

Look at the Circus
NOEL STREATFEILD

Look at Zoos
GERALD DURRELL

Look at Houses
JOHN VERNEY

Look at Canals
L. T. C. ROLT

and there are many others

LOOK
at Churches

ALFRED DUGGAN

Illustrated by RAYMOND BRIGGS

HAMISH HAMILTON
LONDON

First published in Great Britain, 1961
by Hamish Hamilton Ltd.
90 Great Russell Street, London, W.C.1

© 1961 ALFRED DUGGAN

Illustrations © 1961 RAYMOND BRIGGS

PRINTED IN GREAT BRITAIN
BY EBENEZER BAYLIS AND SON, LTD.
THE TRINITY PRESS, WORCESTER, AND LONDON

1

Romanesque

When our Anglo-Saxon ancestors became Christian, about 1,300 years ago, they found they had to build churches. This was quite a new idea to them. As heathens they had worshipped in the open

air. A heathen temple was a house for the god, whose worshippers stood outside. The heathen had a few annual festivals, but nothing like our Christian Sunday.

6

All these new Christians had to meet at the same time, on every Sunday and a number of other holy days during the year, in some building where all could see a priest offering Mass. The building had to keep out the rain, and be a safe storehouse for valuable altar-furniture. It had to be big enough to hold all the people of the parish.

A few churches still remained from the

time of the old Romans, who had been Christian for more than a hundred years before the first Saxons arrived in Britain. We know, for example, that in Canterbury there was an old Roman church, or rather the remains of one. It is still there, and still a church. But St. Martin's has been so thoroughly rebuilt during more than 1,500 years that nowadays it does not look at all Roman. Anyway, these Roman churches were not the kind of thing Saxons could build; the new converts followed a style of their own.

On a small scale they copied some of the details of a Roman shrine. So the style has been called ROMANESQUE, which means "imitation Roman" or "after the Roman manner".

EARLS BARTON CHURCH

Saxons were skilled carpenters, and they liked working in wood. But they were not used to working in stone. When they began shaping stone they imitated woodwork. When they set about building their first churches they made oblong rooms, big enough to house the congregation. At one end, usually the east end because that is nearest to Jerusalem, is a step. On the step is a stone ALTAR.

Now everyone could see what the priest was doing, unless a big window in the eastern wall dazzled the congregation as they looked towards the altar. But normally the windows of a Saxon church are in the other three walls.

These windows are small, like tunnels

WINDOWS AT EARLS BARTON

in the thick walls. This is partly for warmth, since the church has no heating; partly to keep out the rain, since the windows have no glass. The church will be very dark, but that does not matter. The priest can read his book by the light of candles on the altar; the congregation will not mind the gloom, since they cannot read and have no prayer-books.

In building a church of this kind the most difficult bit is the roof. The practical Saxons soon noticed that a church is about the same size as a boat, and that the bottom of a boat, upside down, would make a good enough roof for it. The men who built the boats, called shipwrights, made so many of these wooden roofs that the BODY of a church, the part reserved

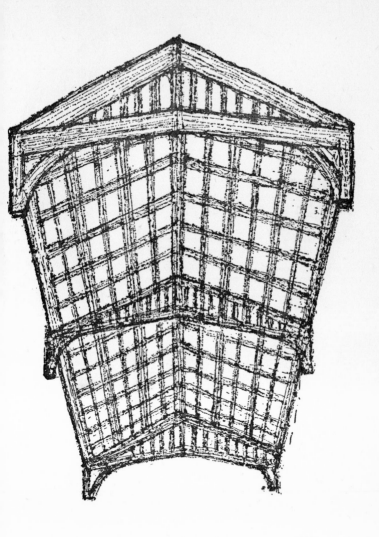

LC-B

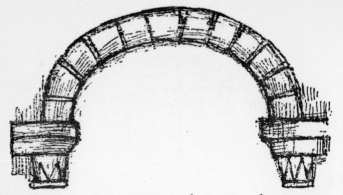

for the congregation, became known as the NAVE (Latin for ship).

At the eastern end the altar was marked off from the nave by a tall semicircular arch resting on pillars. Between the pillars

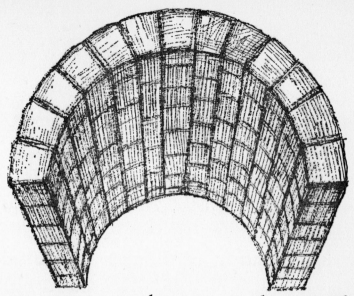

was an open-work screen. So this part of
the church is known as the CHANCEL,
the part beyond the screen. It was often
roofed by extending the chancel-arch east-
ward like the top of a tunnel or the inside
of a barrel, from which this kind of
construction is known as a BARREL-
VAULT. Important churches were

sometimes roofed from end to end with brick or stone barrel-vaults, since a wooden roof easily catches fire.

In the earliest days of Christianity, a group of missionaries would live at the court of each little Saxon king, going out into the villages to offer Mass in barns or in the open air.

A kingdom might have only one genuine church, known as the MINSTER, short for monastery, because most missionaries were monks. There is still a great church in Thanet known simply as Minster, and -minster is tacked on to many other place-names.

The king would pay for the building of minsters. But most of our parish churches were built by private people. A rich man would build a church near his house,

and give the priest some of his land. This was useful and made the rich man feel important.

King Alfred said that anyone who built his own church should rank as a noble, and his sons after him. The rich man appointed the first parish priest, and this right was passed to his sons when he died. Or it might be bought and sold like anything else of value. To this day a private man, the PATRON, appoints, most parish priests. In many country churches you will find a list of patrons and past INCUMBENTS, or parish priests, hanging on a notice board.

There was not much ornament in the fabric of a Romanesque church, though the altar-vessels, the vestments, and even such small things as the book-markers in the big Missal were very beautiful and skilfully made. There might be a band of carving round the outside of the church. Otherwise the chief places for decoration were the round-headed entrance doors and the chancel arch.

These might be surrounded by band after band of carving, Christ in Majesty, the Last Judgement, saints and angels, and other fanciful little figures whose meaning is now lost. Sometimes the carving round arch or door is wider than the opening in the middle. Saxons could carve well on a small scale, but you have to read these decorations bit by bit like a book. You cannot stand back and see the whole mass of carving as one monument.

When you find blocks of stone laid like bricks, alternately lengthways and end on, you will recognize Saxon work; though not all Saxon masonry was laid in this way.

The Romanesque style of building was used throughout the Christian world. When the Normans came in 1066 they also built Romanesque churches. But Normans were energetic and efficient. They organized their estates so that they had plenty of money to spare. They were daring engineers, and on the Continent they had seen the Roman churches of Italy and the copies of those that a great emperor called Charlemagne had built in northern France about the year 800.

The Normans built mighty churches

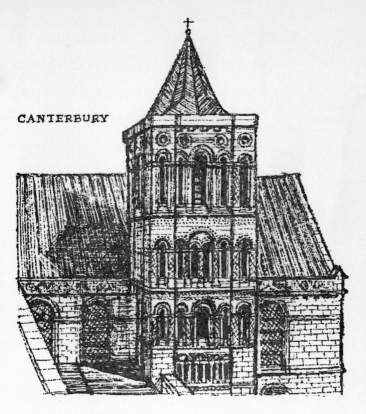

CANTERBURY

and superb cathedrals. Durham is as
splendid as anything built later, and at
Canterbury Romanesque round-headed
arches climb up the great tower to this day.

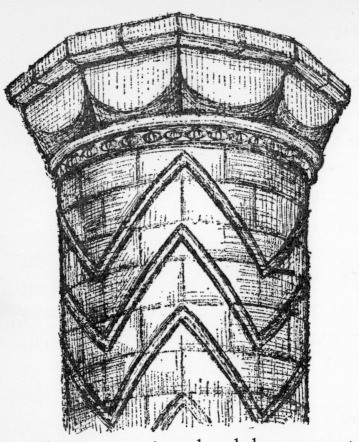

The Normans introduced the ornament
known as the CHEVRON, an open V
like a sergeant's stripes. When you see zig-

zag bands of these running round an arch, or carved on a column, you will know that it was made between 1066 and about 1200 when the Romanesque style went out of fashion.

Norman work that you can still see today is very massive; that is why it has survived. Before a building is begun someone must work out the weight of the roof, and whether the walls will be strong enough to support it. But in the Middle Ages, when our modern Arabic numerals were unknown, it was very hard to do sums in writing. Once you know the trick you can multiply 635 by 48 and get it right. But if you want to multiply DCXXXV by XLVIII you must do it all in your head.

Because they got their sums wrong the Normans often built too lightly. When the building fell down they made it again, with stronger columns and thicker walls. Norman churches, when new, were a patchwork of bright colours. Red or blue chevrons were painted on thin plaster all over the stone columns. Nowadays most of these buildings have been whitewashed, or scraped to the grey stone.

The ceremonies of the Mass had grown more elaborate. In many churches there were a number of priests, who must each offer Mass every morning; so there must be smaller altars at the side of the nave, or in a semicircle at the east end.

Processions went right round the church, so there must be a gangway between the high altar and the eastern wall. Now that Norman engineers have made the churches taller there is room for an east window above the altar, without dazzling the congregation.

In the chancel there may be stone seats, where the clergy can rest during long anthems. Beside the altar there will be a little stone basin and pipe, for the hand-washing during Mass. There will be holy-water stoups by the doors.

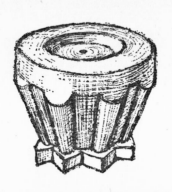

2

Gothic

As the years went by the men who built churches learnt new and better ways. For instance, someone—no one knows who—found a way of using a pointed arch. Between 1175 and 1250 the whole way of designing buildings was changed. Builders found that a pointed arch could be made to any height or any width; by now they had also learned greater skill in handling their materials.

Romanesque builders used any stone they could find near by, and they used it in small shapeless lumps, with a great deal of mortar to hold them together. Gothic masons chose the best stone, and carried it, usually by water, long distances from the quarry. Cotswold stone from above Oxford was used in London, and East Anglia was supplied with Caen stone from far inland in northern France. The stone was cut into large blocks, and each face of it was worked with the chisel.

The new churches were much taller,

LC–C

and much lighter inside. A wall made of big square blocks, accurately fitted, can be thin and still carry a heavy roof that would need a thick wall of rubble and mortar. But instead of a thin wall all the way round, which will still leave the inside dark, you can hold up the roof on piers set at intervals, and in between keep out the weather with large glass windows.

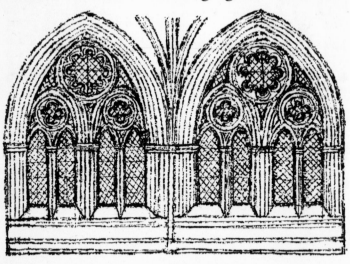

Even the roof need not be thick all over. It is possible to support a slender vault on a few stout ribs, which will lead all the weight down to the piers.

When you look at an old church, ask

yourself this question: Is every bit of the wall carrying the weight of the piece of roof over it, or is the weight carried by a small number of strong piers? This is the chief difference between Romanesque and Gothic churches.

When the new style which we now call EARLY ENGLISH became generally known, every parish wanted to rebuild the local church in this lighter and more

beautiful fashion. That is why few Romanesque churches still remain, and those mostly in poor isolated villages which could never raise the money to build a new church. Yet church-builders, even in wealthy parishes, seldom have all the money they need. If you look carefully, you will often find that Early

English churches were built on the old foundations.

By the thirteenth century England was growing richer. The building of a splendid church was regarded as a good work in itself, and a matter of local pride. At one time it was believed that an enormous church in a small village showed that the village had once been larger. But today people think that the village once happened to be prosperous, and the parishioners built as big as they could afford; not caring that the nave would never be filled, but seeing their fine church as an offering to the Glory of God.

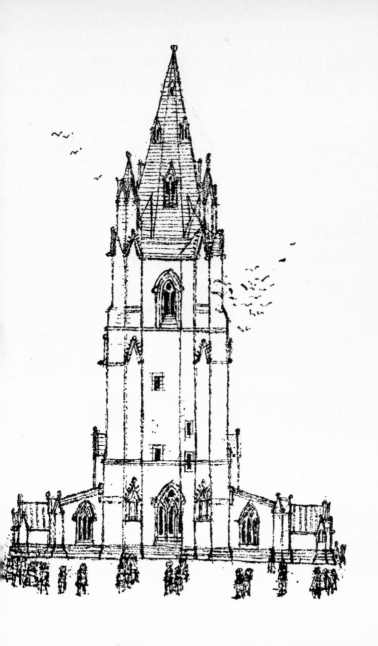

A tall church has no more room for the congregation than a low one; if you want to make it bigger you must make it wide as well. Since it is difficult to design a roof that is both high and wide it was usual to add lower aisles on either side of a tall nave.

But if the windows of a wide church are in the aisles the nave will be dark. To get more light, the builders of an Early English church put windows in the sheer wall of the nave where it rose above the aisles. A range of these windows is known as a CLERESTORY, a bit of Early English spelling that will explain itself if you say it aloud.

A roof always needs repair, and a high Gothic roof is out of reach of ordinary

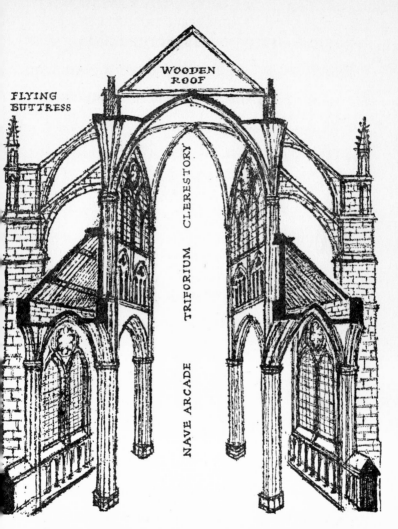

FLYING
BUTTRESS

WOODEN
ROOF

CLERESTORY

TRIFORIUM

NAVE ARCADE

CROSS~SECTION OF A GOTHIC CATHEDRAL

ladders. In the Middle Ages scaffolding was a problem, when the length of a pole was no more than the height of the local trees. So in a tall church you will often find a narrow passage high up in the wall, with arches opening into the nave but no windows to the outside. This is known as a TRIFORIUM.

Singers can be placed in a Triforium. But it is really meant to allow workmen to get easily into the roof of the aisle and with more difficulty into the roof of the nave. The Clerestory was also helpful in this way.

The weight of a roof is always trying to push outwards the supporting walls, and when the roof is very high and the walls very thin this force will be considerable.

To counter it, BUTTRESSES were built against the walls on the outside. To support the higher nave flying buttresses, graceful floating bridges, ran down to meet the walls of the aisles. Flying buttresses, pinnacles, and openwork parapets combined to give the impression of great

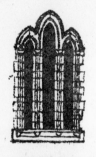

EARLY ENGLISH   DECORATED

height which was the chief aim of Gothic church builders.

Gothic architecture is divided into three styles: EARLY ENGLISH from about 1180 to 1270, DECORATED from 1270 to 1380, PERPENDICULAR from 1380 to the Reformation.

But the styles did not change suddenly

44

from one to another. This is because the aim of the builders had not altered. A church was a place where Mass was offered by the clergy, while laymen looked on and said their prayers. Few laymen could understand the Mass, because it was sung in Latin. All the same, they had to be there, on every Sunday and many holy days. The general appearance of the church was designed to keep them in a religious frame of mind.

For this, churches had to be high. Some Gothic churches are not in fact very tall;

45

but they all *look* high, from the inside. Columns and pointed arches lift your eyes towards heaven. The great windows are meant to be seen from the inside, where the painted glass glows as daylight filters through; the stone tracery shows black against the sky. From outside you cannot make out even the general design of many famous Gothic windows. When these churches were new they were a riot of colour and gilding, making you look up-ward; very often the best painting and carving was in the roof.

The outside may be a muddle, half a dozen varying roof-lines jumbled to-gether. If you already had a Gothic church and wanted to make it bigger and better you added to it; only the old-fashioned

Romanesque churches were deliberately pulled down and built afresh. The usual place for additions was the east end, where another chapel might be built behind the high altar. As a rule this would be dedicated to Our Lady, so that lady-chapel has become the ordinary name for a little chapel jutting out to the east beyond the east end of the church.

Or you might rebuild the nave, leaving unchanged the high altar and chancel, especially if some very holy man was buried there and you did not wish to disturb his tomb. This might have the result that from outside the nave looked taller and more important than the chancel, which annoyed some medieval preachers.

By the late fifteenth century, when

THE CHOIR OF GLOUCESTER CATHEDRAL

Perpendicular was fully developed, some astonishing skyscrapers were built, like the monastic chapel that is now Gloucester Cathedral or the College Chapel at Eton. Buttresses rose to a great height, with between them more glass than wall. The aim seems to have been to enclose as large a space as possible with as little solid masonry as possible; just as modern office-buildings are made from a web of steel girders with mere weatherproof "cladding" in between. The builders of the 1480s dared anything that our engineers dare today, although their churches were made without the machinery that builders have today. All that these medieval builders had were pulleys and wheelbarrows.

3

Inside a Medieval Church

As you approach a church the first thing you notice is the TOWER, perhaps with a spire above it. Though it is the most striking part of the building it has no connection with religion. Bells hang there, and they remind people to come to church at the right time. But in the Middle Ages church bells were used for many other purposes: to call to arms, to give warning of danger, to disperse hailstorms, to drive away witches.

There is no reason why a church should have a tower, but every reason why a village should have one: as a refuge from marauders, or to send signals across country. Probably the villagers built the tower for themselves, and they built it on one end of the church because that was the only building which belonged to all of them.

Often the church was the only public building in the parish, and it was a sort of village hall. The usual way to raise money for any good cause was to hold a "church ale". The ale, given free by the rich, was sold at the church door to be drunk in the churchyard, or, if the weather was bad, even inside the church. Anything that had to be done in public, from a wedding to the election of a mayor, was usually done at the church door.

So when you see notices hanging in the porch you will know that this is the traditional place for them.

Most churches have a big door at the west end that is kept locked. You get in by a smaller door in the south wall, and there may be another opposite it. That is how things have always been. The big west door is open only for great occasions, Palm Sunday processions and the like.

The south door is the normal way into a church. The north door was held to be a bit unlucky, for through it hurried the Devil when he was driven out of a child at baptism.

Over the door, outside, you will see

niches which once held images of the saints. Above the west door there will probably be an elaborate relief, more or less knocked about in past religious quarrels. Inside, a big church or cathedral may give you a clear view up to the high altar and the east window beyond; that is not how it was in the Middle Ages.

A medieval cathedral was cut up into compartments, chiefly because its canons were monks. At dusk, midnight and dawn,

MISERICORD OF SAMSON CARRYING THE GATES OF GAZA

and every three hours during the day, they must meet to sing psalms and prayers. Therefore, west of the high altar is the CHOIR where they sang, an enclosed space screened off from the nave. Inside it seats face one another, with desks in front of them for the psalters. These seats tip up, and the fore-edge is thick and probably carved to form a ledge. A canon standing there for long hours could prop his behind on the ledge and get some rest; hence they are called MISERICORDS, or mercy-seats. Often the carving has nothing to do with religion, but it is very well worth looking at.

Behind the main altar will be an AMBULATORY, a passage for processions going right round the church; and beyond that a lady-chapel, and other chapels. All round the main body of the church will be other little rooms, once used as schoolrooms or the funeral chapels of great families. Nowadays these are VESTRIES, or used for the heating-plant or the electric engine that pumps the organ. In the Middle Ages a school was attached to every cathedral, and the boys were often taught within the church. There was no heating of any kind, except for a rare fireplace in an outer wall.

An ordinary parish church was a simpler building. But even in the plainest old church you will find the remains of one side-altar, needed for the ceremonies of Holy Week. If the screen has been removed, as it should have been, there will

often be a little stair in the thickness of the chancel-arch, now leading nowhere. That was for the cleaners to get at the wooden figures of Our Lord, Our Lady, and St. John, which once stood on top of the screen.

Behind the high altar there may be a piece of wall intricately carved with

CORONATION
OF THE VIRGIN

figures of saints, a kind of permanent
back-drop worked in stone. This is known
as the REREDOS. Usually the originals
have been smashed, but in many churches
they have been replaced by modern copies.

All round you, and especially in the
chancel, will be tombs and memorial inscriptions. Until about two hundred years

THE RESURRECTION

ago it was the custom to bury important people under the floor of the church. The poor were buried in the churchyard, as now, but without tombstones; you will rarely find a monument in any country churchyard older than 1750.

Tombs show the sort of clothes people used to wear, although a gentleman was

shown on his tomb in full armour, even if in life he had never drawn his sword.

The earliest tombs are simple slabs of stone, carved with a cross to show that a Christian lies below. By the twelfth century figures begin to appear on the tomb, showing the dead man lying in state; though it is not certain whether he looked as he is shown on his tomb. But it will certainly show all the emblems of his rank,

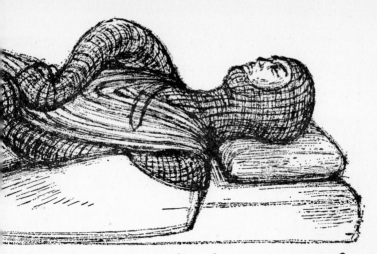

the spurs of a knight, the vestments of a
priest, the crozier of a bishop.

Perhaps the figure will be lying on an
altar, often a sign that the dead man left
money so that Masses should be offered
for his soul in perpetuity. If there is an
inscription you will be unable to read it;
the Latin will be of a kind you do not learn
at school, and the lettering will be strange.

Cheaper memorials were plates of brass,

engraved with a drawing of the dead person. These were not often portraits; for they were made by professionals in big towns, professionals who had never seen the man they were to commemorate. But they will tell you how a man dressed at the time. In the same way alabaster figures of knights, ladies, clerks and bishops were mass-produced near the alabaster quarries. Very often they are elaborate and beautiful carvings, but, of course, they are not accurate portraits of the dead.

Sometimes a tomb was put up long after the death of some nobleman, who had died in disgrace and been buried simply. Thus the tomb of Robert of Normandy in Gloucester Cathedral was carved a century after his death, and shows him in

armour he could never have worn. In some cathedrals the canons put up a series of reclining figures of all their past bishops, long after the holy men were dead and their appearance forgotten.

The Black Death of 1348, a terrible

plague which killed by thousands, made people think much more about death. Some tombs of the fifteenth century are rather horrible. Other tombs of the late Middle Ages are very splendid affairs, with a worldly and cheerful outlook. The dead man and his wife lie in state side by side, she in her best gown and all her jewels, he in complete armour. Round the sides smiling angels hold shields showing the arms of the family and of related families to show how important they were.

After the Reformation altar-tombs are rare, and there are children instead of angels. More often there was just a TABLET on the wall. Tablets for members of the same family were placed together, and in a country church you can often trace every generation of the family who lived in the big house from 1600 to the present day.

Sometimes you may see a HATCH-MENT. This is a board painted with the family arms in full. Within living memory it was hung outside a house whose owner was newly dead, though nowadays the custom has fallen into disuse.

Towards the west end of the church you will find the FONT, which may be older than any part of the present structure. It is at the west end because only Christians should come near an altar; of course a baby cannot be a Christian until it has been baptized. There ought to be a lid on the font, or hanging above it; because in the old days witches and magicians tried to steal the holy water for use in their spells.

4

The Reformation

I have already used the word Reformation, and I should now explain what it means, for it is important. To reform something means to change it for something else that is better. In the sixteenth century, King Henry VIII reformed the Church in

England, although some people do not believe he made it any better. He called himself the Head of the Church in England in place of the Pope in Rome. He destroyed all the monasteries.

Some of the monks in the old monasteries were cruelly treated, and even killed.

The chapels of a few great monasteries were turned into cathedrals; but most of them were pulled down or allowed to fall into ruin.

Objects of gold and silver were confiscated, especially the precious caskets which held relics of the saints. Some church land was taken by the King, and pious people gave no more; for it was evident that all would be taken by the

Crown in the near future. So churches in general were poorer than they had been. But in other ways things went on as before. Every day priests offered Mass, at the high altar and the numerous side-altars. They owed obedience to the King, instead of to the Pope; but their daily lives were not changed.

The great changes were introduced by

the advisers of the boy-King Edward VI. They decreed that all Christians ought to gather together every Sunday to recite prayers, and to listen to very long sermons; but that all other ceremonies and sacraments were no longer needed. Even praying in church was a matter for Sundays only, and should not occur on weekdays.

There were no more Masses, though three or four times a year the Communion service was read at a wooden table. So the stone altars were destroyed, images of saints were smashed, stained glass windows were broken, as were screens and any other ornament that might carry the forbidden crucifix. But the tombs of ordinary men who had never

been venerated as saints were not disturbed.

Many churches became bare whitewashed halls, with plain glass in the windows. There would be a pulpit for sermons, and a movable wooden table stored normally in a corner and brought into the middle of the nave for the rare Communions. Some Reformers even wore their hats in church, to show that it was just a building like any other.

That was what the government wanted. But Edward's reign was short and disturbed, and his advisers had other worries besides religion. In the big towns, and in districts where the common people wanted the Reformation, these changes were carried out in full; but in many country districts old forbidden ornaments survived. Then after King Edward came Queen Mary, who brought back the Pope, and Mass in Latin, and all the old ways.

After Mary's death her sister, Queen Elizabeth I, set up the Church of England with the doctrines and Articles which now exist. But things were not quite the same. As in King Edward's day, the object of

EDWARD VI   MARY I

going to church on Sunday, which everyone had to do or pay a fine or go to
prison, was to hear English prayers read
from a book, and a sermon. On weekdays the church was locked.

At the present time the only reminder of
the constant prayer of medieval England
is the daily service held in every cathedral.

Communion was celebrated at a wooden
table set up in the nave. No vestments
were worn, though some clergy wore a

surplice while reading from the Book of Common Prayer, and took it off to preach in a black gown.

Services could be very long. A sermon lasting three hours was not unknown. So for the first time proper seating was provided for the whole congregation. As a rule the squire, who still appointed the parson as his predecessor had done in the days of King Alfred, sat in a square box pew, where he could see the head of the preacher in the pulpit but no other member of the congregation could see *him*. Yeomen and tenant-farmers built themselves lesser pews, and there were simple benches for the poor.

Since everyone had to go to church, and the population was increasing, some churches became uncomfortably crowded. So wooden galleries were built at the west end of the churches. You can still see some of these galleries today, and they are well worth looking at, for many of them are beautifully carved.

By law, the royal arms were displayed somewhere in the church to show that the king was the head of the church. Since images of the saints were not allowed, any religious paintings on the walls had to be covered with whitewash. But to avoid the dullness of completely blank walls very often the Ten Commandments, the Lord's Prayer, and the Apostles' Creed were written up in English.

When William Laud became Archbishop of Canterbury, in the reign of Charles I, he tried to bring back some of the old customs. As Chancellor of Oxford he had already caused great excitement by putting up a statue of Our Lady over the door of the University Church. Now in every church he tried to get the Communion Table moved to the east end. Congregations were ordered to stand up to recite the Creed, and to receive Com-

KING CHARLES I

munion kneeling in a row; instead of sitting round the Table with their hats on according to the custom of the more ardent Reformers.

Laud's changes met with great opposition, and helped to bring about the terrible Civil War, when Englishmen fought against Englishmen. By the end of that war, in 1646, all the churches in England had fallen into the hands of the winning Roundheads, and were altered to what they wanted. More stained glass was smashed, surviving images of the saints were broken; in addition the font was removed, and the organ put out of action by puncturing the bellows. (In the Middle Ages organs had been rare because they were difficult to make; during the sixteenth century they had become more common.) The parish church was again made as much as possible into a plain preaching-hall.

In 1660, Charles II came back as king; and the Church of England was restored as it had been under Archbishop Laud and is now. Churchwardens routed out the old font, the Communion Table went back permanently to the east end, and once more the royal arms hung on the wall. Very often a tablet was put up somewhere to commemorate this happy restoration, with the names of the churchwardens who had arranged it.

When you visit an old church you can carry out an interesting piece of detection. Note to what extent the orders of the central government were obeyed as from time to time they came down from London. You will learn at the same time whether the extreme Reformers were strong in the neighbourhood, or whether the people clung to the old ways. In some remote parts of Wales, for example, screens still stand in the churches complete with crucifix and figures of Our Lady and St. John, contrary to the orders of Edward VI.

If the royal arms have the Tudor Dragon of Elizabeth I as supporter, instead of the Scottish unicorn, they must have hung in the church without a break since 1603, even though the Roundheads ordered their removal.

Always note the form of the royal arms, which will tell you when they were put up. Stuarts quartered the Scottish Lion, William III displayed his ancestral arms on a little shield in the centre, the House of Hanover added their White Horse, George III dropped the French Lilies. The arms of Charles II indicate that the parish was strongly Cavalier, those of William III that it was Whig. A Jacobite parish would be reluctant to display Hanoverian arms, and would patch up the old Stuart ones.

In general the remote countryside did not care for change; while in big towns the government enforced its rules with a strong hand. If you look alertly you will find fascinating survivals: images of saints which were saved by being buried in time of danger, stone altars which were disguised by putting a wooden Communion Table over them, stone coffins of holy men and venerable stone fonts which in bad times were taken out of the church and hidden in farm-yards as feeding-troughs for animals, though the whole parish knew where they were and kept them undamaged until it was safe to bring them back.

Or you may find, especially in a town which flourished in the seventeenth century, a church still as it was in 1661: no images, a wooden Communion Table standing on four legs at the east end without any disguise of altar-frontal, the pulpit as the central object in the church, long inscriptions hanging on the walls as the only form of decoration, windows of plain glass, severe uncomfortable benches —and somewhere tucked away under the tower a small and niggling copy of the arms of Charles II as the only thing that would seem strange to a chaplain of Cromwell's army if he should come back to revisit it.

Both forms of survival, the old pre-Reformation objects lovingly preserved and the accessories of the vanished Commonwealth defiantly displayed, remind us of the continuity of parish life.

ST. PAUL'S 5 CATHEDRAL

Churches of the Last 300 Years

In the century after the Restoration there was a great deal of church-building. This was done partly to repair the damage done in the Civil War, partly to replace churches damaged by fire (especially the Great Fire of London in 1667). New churches were also needed just because there were more people. These new churches were quite different, inside and out, from the old ones.

In the Cotswolds, to the east of Bristol, Gothic churches were still built, with door-cases or windows in conventional Tudor Perpendicular. But mere craftsmen would not be left to design a whole church on their own. Now there were architects. These architects tried to copy the great Italian builders of the sixteenth century, who had themselves been trying to copy the monuments of pagan Rome.

The new churches were built for the new form of religion. The people wanted to hear a preacher who stood in a pulpit facing the nave, instead of seeing a priest who stood at the altar with his back to them. Compared with the old church, this was more like a theatre or a lecture room. The ideal is a wide square nave, with perhaps a gallery at the west end to hold the overflow if the church is crowded.

Sir Christopher Wren made the best models by his rebuilding of St. Paul's and the City parish churches after the Great Fire. St. Paul's is a Roman building, supported by correct columns of the ancient Roman kind, roofed with a mighty Roman dome. The whole church is centred on the pulpit, so that a great crowd can follow one service, all seeing and hearing everything done by the

ST. MARTIN'S IN THE FIELDS

minister. This was very different from the old days before the Reformation when six priests would be doing different things in different corners of a long building.

Other town churches were not so grand as St. Paul's; but on their smaller scale they were made after the same fashion. Sometimes the outside is more imposing than the inside, as at St. Martin's in the Fields, in London. St. Martin's was paid for by the people, who gave the money.

In general, a medieval church was built from the centre outwards, the centre being some holy shrine or at least a venerated altar. The outer walls were less important, although above them there often towered a lofty spire. The higher the spire, the grander was the church.

In the eighteenth century, on the other hand, many churches were built to be seen from across the street, and less care was devoted to the inside. Eighteenth-century churches often looked just like the market and the town hall.

In the country not so many new churches were needed, but the few that were built are often remarkable. The reason for their building was usually that the squire had enlarged his house and park, and by a private Act of Parliament had removed the village to a more convenient site (more convenient for the squire, of course). Then he would build the new church at his own expense, either to his own design, or on the advice of a well-known architect.

These churches were built to the Glory of God; for it was still a God-fearing age. But the glory of the squire came a very good second, and the rest of the parishioners were apt to be overlooked. The squire's great pew is furnished like a comfortable drawing-room, with its own fireplace and a table for his hat and books. Above all, the walls of the church are a background for memorials of the squire's ancestors and relations.

These memorials tell us about the dead man's career in detail, any appointments he held, his noble connections by blood or marriage. They are more often in English than in Latin. They provide interesting reading, and the carved decoration is often very good of its kind.

By the nineteenth century the population of most English towns had become much greater. There were many new parishes on the edges of the towns, and these were often poor. At this time Gothic was considered the only style suitable for

a sacred building. Some nineteenth-century churches are absurd and fanciful copies of Gothic, but as the fashion took hold Early English, Decorated, and Perpendicular were seriously studied and accurately reproduced. At the present day what is called Gothic Revival is taken very seriously as an architectural style.

It seems to me that the revivalists made one serious mistake. They knew that real Gothic churches had been colourful when they were new, and they wished to provide the vivid reds and blues. But they were inclined to be frightened of wall-painting, and relied instead on coloured floor-tiles and coloured masonry, which do not produce the same effect.

By the end of the nineteenth century archaeology and art-history were beginning to be considered more important than theology; if something odd and interesting was discovered in a medieval church it was often put on display even though it might be against the doctrines of the Church of England.

A typical instance is the wall-painting in Eton College Chapel. These pictures were painted in the fifteenth century in honour of Our Lady; and covered up by the Reformers because they disapproved of such honour being given to her. In the mid-nineteenth century they were discovered in the course of repairs; but kept under whitewash because they were considered Popish, as indeed they are. During the 1920s they were uncovered and restored as interesting examples of fifteenth-century art. Nobody worried about the contradiction between the paintings and the doctrines taught in the chapel.

From time to time new churches are built, quite unlike anything that has gone before. Architects and builders need no longer work only in stone and brick since concrete and other new materials can be made in any size or shape. There is no reason why these new churches should not be beautiful, and it is silly to sneer at them simply because they are strange.

But all parish churches have something in common, whether they were built under King Alfred or under Queen Elizabeth II.

On the Communion Table will be a cross, because Christ is worshipped here; in the porch will be secular official notices, because the Church of England is the Established Church; on the walls will be memorials of the dead of the recent wars, whether or no these men ever entered a church while they were alive, because this building is the spiritual centre of the community.

THE END